Bits & Pieces

Naomi Smith

Copyright © 2014 by Naomi Smith

All rights reserved. No part of this publication may be reproduced, distributed, or transmitted in any form or by any means, including photocopying, recording, or other electronic or mechanical methods, without the prior written permission of the publisher, except in the case of brief quotations embodied in critical reviews and certain other noncommercial uses permitted by copyright law.

ISBN-10: 0985902876
ISBN-13: 978-0-9859028-7-2

Authored by Naomi Smith
https://www.facebook.com/pages/Bits-Pieces/781078398629700?pnref=lhc.recent

Published by Broken Publications
www.BrokenPublications.com

Edited by Jennifer-Crystal Johnson
www.JenniferCrystalJohnson.com

Book cover design & layout by Jennifer-Crystal Johnson
www.JenniferCrystalJohnson.com

Printed in the United States.

A
Pacific Northwest
Publisher

www.BrokenPublications.com

For my mom - my hero.
You are my rock, supporting me and encouraging me
to be myself no matter what.

Table of Contents

Let Me Out	11
Rainy Weather	12
Grasshopper	13
Shiver	14
Flutter	15
Sense	16
You	17
Cold Weather	18
Kidnap Me	19
A Moment of Beauty at the Lake	21
First Crush	22
Who Bullies the Bullies?	23
Bleeding Humanity	24
Distress Signal	25
Elemental Prayer	26
Untitled	27
My Love Affair with the Moon, pt. 1	31
Fever Dream	32
Shadows and Light	33
Big Water	34
Field of Dreams	35
Veil	39
Ritual	40
Hiding the Rust	41
Leaves	42
Goodbyes	43
Music is Your Only Friend	44
Nowhere	45
My Love Affair with the Moon, pt. 2	46
Young Lust	47
Peace of Mind	48
The Underground	49
The Romeo and Juliet Deviation	50
A Cricket's Song	51
Careful, Don't Cut Too Deep	53
Storm Front	54
Night	55

Welcome to the Hellmouth	58
Wake Up	59
Love Immortal	60
We All Fall Down	61
This is Not the Path I Sought	63
Descent	64
Blue	65
I Don't Have To	66
Sensitivity	67
Bits & Pieces	68
The Morning After	69
Shadow on the Wall	70
Falling	71
Just Me and the Frogs	72
Soul Erotica	73
She	75
Succubus	76
Downward Spiral	77
This is Not the Road I Thought	78
Enemy	79
Damaged	80
Cuts	81
A Denny's Poem	82
A Breakthrough	83
This is Not the Dream I Bought	84
The Cycle	85
Coffee Camping Solo	86
Realization and Denial	87
I Sense Something is Amiss	88
Gaslight	89
Hindsight (is Always 20/20)	90
Just a Fever of Fate I've Caught	91
Restless	92
Free	93
Moving On	94
La passion	95
Chameleon Girl	96
Sanctuary	97
The Compatibility Culmination	98

Pestilence	99
Spark	100
Hollow Dolly	101
Skinny Bitch	102
Dad	103
I Hope it Was Worth It	104
Beautiful Host	105
About the Author	106

Let Me Out

Trapped in this
      equilibrium
      of boredom,
Unable to amuse myself
      with something exciting;
My ennui a tranquilizer
      designed to keep me
      sedated—
Trapped in a prison
      without bars or restraints,
Yet unable to escape
      the barrier…
My only relief is the realms
      that my imagination
Takes me to.
Someone let me out!

Rainy Weather

Rainy weather everywhere…
Tears fall endlessly,
Like a flash flood
In the land of Betrayal.

Rainy weather today…
Sweat falls to the ground
Like a salty summer shower
In the land of Work.

Rainy weather all day…
Spit falls from the dark sky
Like a cold winter storm
In the land of Scorn.

Rainy weather is all you see,
Rainy weather is all you hear,
Rainy weather is all you feel,
In the land of Opportunity.

Grasshopper

Colors of sickly yellow, faded red,
        vibrant orange, and leaf green
Painted onto a shell armor,
        strong as a brick wall.
It moves slowly, nonchalantly,
        as if it has nowhere important
        to be at any given time,
Yet catapults quickly into the air,
        as if it had strong, steel springs
        for legs.
Its visage hideous and cruel,
Its jaws open and ready to clamp down
        on anything that moves
        so much as an inch,
Its stance, ready to attack its foe
        if provoked…
Yet it is harmless, but to green foliage.

Shiver

A chill…
Icy fingers make frozen trails
Up and down my spine.
Whispers travel through my nerves,
Throughout by body.
I shake…
A convulsion.

One.

Solitary.

Shiver.

A ghost of a promise of the past.
A silent kiss brought on by
        a cool breeze.
The base of my spine ripples,
Trembles
With the ecstasy of
The silent, single quake
Traversing the contours of
My body.

Flutter

What is it that I feel
When we touch?
That intense spark of electricity
That drives me crazy.

What is it that I feel
When our lips meet?
That flighty tingle
That tugs at the pit of my stomach.

What is it that I feel
Every time I see you?
That makes my heart pound
With the fury of a stampede.

What is it that I feel?

Sense

I hear...
The conversing of birds in
      the midday sun,
The ding of an open car door
      down the street,
The whispers of the breeze
      as it whistles through the trees,
The sound of leaves scraping between the
      weight of shoe-clad feet and
      cement sidewalk,
The rustle of lizards through the
      green, green grass as they
      scurry from my steps,
The boom of music from cars as they
      pass by my block,
The thoughts, the wishes,
      the dreams of those whose
      eyes I look into,
The silent conversations of our souls
      as our eyes meet,
The void of unconsciousness as it
      perches outside my window of vision,
The knocks of my personal demons
      as they rap ever so lightly—like a
      taunting feline kiss—and pound
      so frightfully loud; like tyrants
      invading kingdoms, knocking, rapping,
      pounding relentlessly upon my being.

You

met you
knew you
humored you

                        liked you
                       dated you
                      kissed you

                                               fought you
                                           punched you
                                                   bit you

touched you
caressed you
soothed you

                     possessed you
                        shook you
                       slapped you

                                             owned you
                                             called you
                                           stalked you

followed you
attacked you
killed you

                        loved you
                          let you
                        lost you

Cold Weather

It slips in at night
      like a silent cockroach
      in a dirty kitchen.
It fills every empty void
With a bitter chill.
It bites at my flesh like piranha,
Tearing at my skin.
The icy wind claws at my cheeks
Like a knife through raw meat…
My skin becomes a beaten red,
      and then the freezing, bruised
      blue and purple.
The trees bend and sway to an
      invisible rhythm, a silent song
      that echoes through my soul.
The cold weather grips my existence and
      purges my mind, clearing it in
      the breeze like leaves blown down
      a dark, deserted street.

Kidnap Me

Kidnap me…
Take me blindfolded
To your hideaway.
Take me far, far away
From the bustle
Of the city streets,
From the honking horns
And blaring stereo systems,
From the shouts of anger
And the cries of pain.

Take me to a place
Where the cool,
Sweet summer wind blows
And the trees sway
With the sound
Of the crisp bluegrass trill,
And the people are hypnotized
By the beautiful soul
Of real music.

Take me to a place
Where the shouts are joyous
And the only cries of pain
Are from our feet,
Sore from dancing!

Take me to a place
Where our spirits soar
With the twang
Of a steel guitar.

Drag me away
From this labyrinth
Of zigzag streets
To a place
Where, as far as the eye can see,

There is nothing but saw grass
Swaying with the music made
By the hidden night creatures.

Take me to a place
Where the souls of legends
Soar to the stars.

Kidnap me…
Take me away at once—
I will be your willing captive.

A Moment of Beauty at the Lake

Fine wisps of fluffy, airy cotton candy
Slice through psychedelic kaleidoscope
        colors of a transparent sheen.
They melt and are transformed into
        blazing pinks, bruised purples,
        brilliant blues, and shimmery
        oranges, all mixed with golden light
        like honey.
A red-orange orb slides through an
        atmosphere of poetic light.
Insignificant,
        yet that which is routine; so meaningless,
Can be the most profound occurrence to be
        witnessed by
A soul of such omneity that even an
        event so prehistoric can mean
        the world; can be of such breathtaking
        beauty that time—even having such
        eternal routine as he—stops altogether
        so that the instance, that which is
        there and gone in the blink of an eye,
Can remain painted in memory for
        an eternity.

First Crush

A smile…
but is it real?
A touch…
but do you feel?
A look…
a hungry soul's meal.
A word…
my heart it could steal.

I'm fighting this battle
with all my might.

A spark…
a light…
I won the game,
but lost the fight.

Who Bullies the Bullies?

So, what's with your kind?

You rummage to find
The insignificance
      of maudlin fools
That you love to hate,
But do you love your-
      self anymore?
Does your self-esteem level
      rise a notch
Every time you drag
      someone else down?
What do you feel when you see
      someone cry
So that you don't have to?
Does it make you feel
      better about yourself
When you see someone
      more miserable than you?
Does it make you smile when you see
      someone so terribly helpless,
Locked up inside themselves
      in the dark corners of hell?

You choose the path dividing
Yourself from your conscience,
Taking advantage of despair.
Who will be the next in line?

Bleeding Humanity

The sun and moon,
they speak to me
of lives past and things to come.
I have seen a desolate future
destroyed by Man and his
      incomprehensible ignorance;
greed, hate, indifference
wrought upon this world
      by its very own "protectors."
I cast my soul into a spell
      to heal this
bleeding humanity.

Distress Signal

I want to get your attention.
I want you to know who I am inside,
      what I hear,
      what I see.
I want you to notice what I am becoming.
So…

I'll scream at you until my face turns purple,
      until my eyes sweat,
      until my throat bleeds,
      until my head explodes.
I'll scream at you until your eardrums burst,
      until the moon falls from the sky and crushes me,
      until the world falls up,
      until water becomes blood.
I'll scream at you until you listen to me,
      until you know who I am,
      hear what I hear,
      see what I see…
Until you notice what I have become.

Elemental Prayer

Fire element burning bright,
Bless me as I sleep tonight.
Keep me cozy, safe, and warm;
Shield me from a nightmare's harm.

Element Earth, sturdy and true,
Protect me from wicked screams
All night long, I ask of you;
Allow me none but pleasant dreams.

Water element, deep and calm,
Guard me 'til the coming dawn.
Watch over me as I sleep tonight;
Lead me on the path that's right.

Element Air, wild and free,
Pass your blessings on to me.
Element Air, cool and crisp,
Protect me from a nightmare's kiss.

Untitled

I am the face in your dreams
      that you can't quite remember
      no matter how hard you try.
I am the trees above and
      the grass beneath your feet.
I am the star-studded sky that
      you gaze up at
      when all the world's asleep.
I am the coffin in which
      you lay to rest your
      deceased.
I am the blisters on your skin from
      the sweltering summer sun.
I am the invisible kiss of a breeze while
      you lay out and catch falling stars.
I am the worms inside the apple
      that has returned to the earth.
I am the fragrant blooms in your garden
      that turn toward the morning light.
I am the swagger in the step of the drunken
      old vagrant that pushes past and laughs
      in your face, with reeking breath
      and fouled clothes.
I am the lost soul that soars through the skies
      and passes through you like
      a needle through cloth.
I am the sand in the bag of the
      Sandman as he puts the world
      to sleep.
I am the rock that you skip over the
      surface of the waters of time.

I am joy
I am pain
I am happiness
I am depression
I am longing

I am obsession
I am anger
I am hate
I am grief
I am fear

I am the need to change.
I am the fire that burns
    within the souls of each
    and every one of us.
I am the right choice.
I am the wrong choice.
I am the path that divides
    good and bad.
I am the mischievous gleam
    in the eyes of a young child.
I am the determined look of
    a struggling mother.
I am the precious moments that
    fill your lives.
I am the bump or creak or
    moan that haunts you in the night.
I am the lightning bolt that
    splits your backyard tree
    in half.
I am the jealousy that devours
    you bit by bit.
I am the heat that
    boils your blood when
    you are belittled.
I am the selfish instinct for
    survival that makes
    liars of us all.

I am the believer
I am the atheist
I am the agnostic
I am the witch

I am the poetry that
    floats through the sky and
    among the clouds at sunset.
I am the crack of the bat
    when a home run is hit.
I am the shouts of glee when the
    sight of first snow promises
    a day off from school.
I am the bubbles that float to
    the surface of a fish tank
    with no fish.

I am the abused
I am the abuser
I am the addict
I am the drug
I am the criminal
I am the victim
I am insecurity
I am apathy

I am the bold sunrise
    over tree tops of green glory.
I am the reflection in the mirror
    of time.
I am the words that flow
    from this pen.
I am the vibrations of ecstasy that
    course through the nerves of
    every breathing soul.
I am the chill in the
    cool autumn air.
I am the scrape of shoes upon
    gravel as pedestrians shuffle
    across the streets of nowhere.
I am the time that is wasted
    procrastinating the things that
    should be done yesterday.
I am the scrapes and bruises

       on the body of a careless child.
I am the fairy that tugs at
       your eyelids when you
       can barely keep them open.
I am the spark that sets a forest
       fire ablaze in the hearts
       of young lovers.

I am the insanity that overwhelms
       the feeble-minded.
I am the cynicism in the old.
I am the elegance of a graceful
       animal running through its
       territory.
I am the pride of a patriot that swells
       his chest, great and golden.
I am the will to survive.
I am life itself.
I am everything that has
       no meaning to anyone.
I am anything that is
       Everything.
I am anything, and everything,
       and possibly nothing
       at all.

My Love Affair with the Moon, pt. 1

I love the beach at night:
the white sand
reflecting the moon;
the crystals
sparkle like diamonds;
the bonfire flames
warm my skin
with their orange flicker;
the fire fairies
dance through licking tongues.
Burning wood
snaps, crackles,
burns red,
and fades to grey.
The night sky is alive with
glittering eyes
in a place where time,
all thought,
has no meaning.

Fever Dream

I once saw a caterpillar
    sitting on a daisy.
He said to me: "This weather is enough
    to make me crazy.
I sit upon this flower
    every single morning,
Whether it is sunny
    or whether it is storming,
And still, the sun, it rises
    each and every day;
It's full of great surprises
    in which I love to play.
The sun falls upon me,
    bakes me like toast;
It begins to get hot,
    so I start to roast.
Just when the heat becomes too much,
    clouds roll in on wheels of air
Like a finger's cooling touch.
    Oh! What a playful pair!
Rain falls onto my parched, dry skin
    as if answering my prayer;
Drops so tiny, oh so small,
    making the day pleasant and fair."

"Time for you to wake up, lazy,"
    said to me the caterpillar, small,
Sitting there upon a daisy…
    I guess he wasn't real after all.

Shadows and Light

The sonnets of
Mother Nature begin
With the rapturous
      flare
Of the early morning sunrise;
The heavens alight with
The fire of the gods,
      foreshadowing the
      harsh day ahead,
And end with the
      dying embers of
An industrious blaze,
Illuminating the nearly
      twilight skies
And painting the tapestry
      of clouds
With their fading colors.

Big Water

Who else saw
        that glorious sunset,
Perfect as no other could be?
Who remembered the whispers
        on the ancient breeze
That floated across that
        fresh-water sea?
Who closed their eyes
        and made a wish
Upon a snow-white
        heron's shriek?
Who splashed through the
        shallow beach waters
And took imaginary
        snap-shot photos?
Who gazed upon
        the rising moon
And talked of things
        that only we could see?
No one but you and me.

Field of Dreams

The chilly autumn wind whipped
        through the trees as we walked
        down the deserted street.
Hand in hand we strolled, listening
        to howls and whispers,
        our heartbeats in our ears.
Your hand was warm and clammy
        against mine as they swung freely
        between us.
Then I broke the silence and asked:
        "If I didn't care enough to tell you the truth,
        would you believe my dishonest words?"
You thought for a few steps and then
        replied: "No."
When I asked you why, you told me that
        you knew me better than that,
And you knew that I didn't doubt you
        for a minute.
More silence as we crossed the old dirt road
        and headed into the field of dreams,
        just down the street from my house.

We pushed through the flimsy stalks until we
        found our home-made crop circle.
There, we spread out my ever-resting grandmother's
        quilt that was passed down to me
        just a few years ago.
We lay out under the stars and watched
        the wind sway the surrounding field.
Love was falling all around us that night
        as we wished upon shooting stars
        and made love under the moon.
The heady scent of cannabis mingled with
        our sweat and the fresh air
That swirled around our bodies
        under the moonlight and stardust
        as the midnight fairies buzzed and

    twirled and swooped
Down through our tangled hair and reflected
    their fluorescence in our eyes.
I saw the passion and desire burning
    in your soul that night,
     and you knew I felt the same.
The moon was a blinding white against
    a shroud of indigo
As I lay on my back, staring up
    at my own reflection cast in that
    great, full orb of light.
Questions and answers burned my soul
    that night, like a forest fire raging
    through my body.
I felt every tremor of thunder and
    every bolt of lightning blaze through
    my brain, my heart, my soul,
    my entire body.
I looked at you and saw that you
    felt the same.
For us, everything changed that night
    and would never be the same,
For dreams come true in our
    field of dreams.

But...
Then I found that nightmares come true
    in that field of dreams,
For nightmares are dreams, too.
We continued to visit the field of dreams together
    until the day that the spirits
    took you away from me.
You departed so horribly, I could not
    bear to watch,
Yet I was unable to look away.
Your face distorted, your body so
    wretchedly twisted,
Dissolved right before my eyes.

I think of you now, after all
    these years have passed,
And I remember the love
    that we shared,
The color of your eyes so vivid
    in my memory.
The smoothness of your skin and
    the weight of you and
The way that your gentle fingers brushed
    lightly over my skin
    and through my hair.
I lay at night in our field of dreams
    and I feel your presence beside me,
        in your place on my grandmother's quilt.
I hear you whisper to me
    through the breeze that you
    will always be here,
    waiting for me.
Waiting for the night that
    the spirits take me away.

So easy to forget, that which
    is in the past.
But after all these years, so
    many decades,
I have not forgotten the field of dreams.
I have not forgotten you or the
    midnight fairies that still dance
    through my tangled hair
When I lie down on my grandmother's
    quilt, now tattered and worn.
I have not forgotten the stars of
    love in your eyes.
You have always had the largest
    piece of my heart;
No one else has come close.
Although I have learned to love others,
    time has taken a toll
    on my memory,

For I have forgotten every face
        but yours.
It is forever etched into the
        stone wall of my heart.

This morning I awoke in the
        field of dreams,
And I knew that tonight I would
        finally join you.
I would become a dream the way
        you did all those years ago.
At last, the spirits would have
        mercy upon my old and weathered eyes,
        and bless me with the sight
        of you once again.
And I knew that once I have become
        a dream,
Another pair of empty souls
        will be filled with each other.
We will watch them, and teach them,
        and love them.
We will send the midnight fairies
        to twirl through their hair
        and weave their spell
        around them as they once did us.
Our field of dreams will once again
        spin its web of reverie…
And nightmares….

Veil

An ache…
Like an ember in my heart,
A leaden weight.
It lingers like a haze after a storm,
A fog over my eyes,
Forbidding me to see the beauty in the world.
I cannot pierce this black veil,
Though I struggle.
I feel as though I'm drowning
In a sea of my own sorrow.
My soul is sick…
It may be dying.

Ritual

Cast the circle
Then hold hands;
Round and round
The witches dance.
Twirling sky-clad,
Hands held high,
Swirling with
The fireflies.

Fire, Water,
Earth, and Air,
Spirit guardians
Standing there.
Chant the words
Of Wiccan song;
The path of light
Will do no harm.

Hiding the Rust

Standing in the rain
of rejection,
The raindrops mingle
with my tears
And soak my hair through.

By any chance, am I
the least bit sane?

The mud puddles of love
are flooded, overflowing,
And I splash around in them
like a grounded duck.
I mill about in agony,
waiting for time to heal
The grievous wound of
my broken heart.

But will all the time in
the universe heal the damage
That has been inflicted
upon my fragile soul?

Like the weather, love has…
changed.
Dark and oppressive thunderheads
threaten to spill their
Sorrow upon the world,
like a carpet of ancient dust
Covering the floor and
hiding the rust.

Leaves

Leaves fall
To catch you and I
As you tumble me into dead and
        dying foliage
Of muddy browns and brilliant oranges,
        rich reds and translucent yellows.
They crunch and crackle and
        whisper to each other,
Secrets of our love affair.
They tangle themselves in our hair
        to later be tenderly
Plucked out by our gentle fingers.
They carpet the ground beneath
        our feet, hiding its treasures
        from our eyes.
They chatter and swish as our
        shod and bare feet
        snake through them.
They fall upon our heads, like
        New Year's confetti, joy and
        celebration in a season of their own.

Goodbyes

Goodbyes are not forever,
But farewells may very well be;
So say not farewell
To everything that ye know of here,
Neither say goodbye to anything
For goodbyes last much too long.
Merely say you'll be back someday
And be sure to attempt a return.

Fear not what lies ahead for ye;
'Tis awaiting thee with arms stretch'd open.
Play their games by thy rules
And be proud of what ye are;
Trip not o'er bad words ye may receive,
But return them with a kind word or blessing.
Be patient, dear friend,
And ye shall have that which ye desire.

Love comes not from the mind
But from the heart,
And those that love with their hearts
Truly love.
A true friend will love thee
Whether or not ye be a beau,
For the beauty itself lies within the heart
And one who loves thy heart is truly a friend.

Music is Your Only Friend

When the music's over,
Turn off the disco ball
For the mirrors are
No longer reflecting.
When the time has come
To say goodnight,
Make a wish
As you shut off the light.
The moonlight shines
In the pools of your eyes;
Strobe light pulses in
A sea of dark.
When the time comes
To say your prayers,
Put in a good word
For the sake of me.
This nightmare, a quaking shiver,
A vision of things to come.

Nowhere

I dreamt that I left town
        and went nowhere.
I left behind
Empty promises and broken hearts;
The sea was pink and the sunset blue.
I sat against the earth and
        watched for hours.
Brightly colored crabs turned into
        seagulls and flew away,
Just like my hopes and dreams.

I dreamt I went to the big city
And all the cars flew around on
        invisible highways.
I could see inside peoples' minds,
But there was nothing in them.
They were as hollow as the steel drums
        that rang down the street.
And every night I came home
To listen to static on the radio
And read books with blank pages.

I dreamt that I moved to a farm
        in the middle of nowhere.
There, I could hear the music
        on my radio,
And read the words in my books,
And watch the sun sink into
        the earth.
There, I could sleep peacefully
And hope my hopes,
And dream my dreams,
And never lose them again.

My Love Affair with the Moon, pt. 2

The moon… reflecting in the water,
The sea foam bobbing
With the gentle undulation
Of the waves
Shining on the beach.
The white sand makes
My pale feet seem dark.
Dancing along the shore,
The waves tug playfully
      at my ankles,
Twirling faster and faster,
Pulling the wind along with me,
My soul soaring with the Cosmos
As I lay in the sand.
Gazing up at glittering velvet,
My eyes grow heavy
And I dream.

Young Lust

I am entranced,
Entangled,
Enraptured
By what some
Call love,
An infinite
Understatement
When one is caught
In the midst
Of our presence.

Peace of Mind

A myriad
Of wildflowers thrust from
      the earth,
Straining to reach the sky;
Their scents
And hues blend in dizzying ecstasy.
Rolling hills
Of a magnificent green
Are ripples in a vast carpet,
An ancient tree
Here and there.
The peaks of clouds at sunset
Are of the purest gold.
The sky explodes with brilliant splashes
Of rich, deep color that play
Across my field of vision,
Tantalizing my senses, exhilarating me,
Offering me peace of mind.

The Underground

An uprooted tree stump…
An empty hole where
        its roots used to be.
A chill wind…
Snaking its way through the
        leaves of desolate trees
Scattered here and there.

Broken bottles, broken bones;
Broken hearts, broken homes.

Bullet casings lying around for
        little children to play with.
A torn flag flaps in the breeze
        against a cloud-spattered sky.
The birds don't even sing anymore.

Sticks and stones may break bones,
        but hateful words leave
        scars on souls.
The fields frozen with greed that
        falls upon them like a
        midnight frost.
The trees sag and sigh with hopelessness.

The street lights don't even
        work anymore…
They've all been shot out.

The Romeo and Juliet Deviation

How does one compare
The love one feels for another
To that of love praised in poetry?
When we are mere mortals,
Struggling for survival,
While lovers in yarns
Are immortal,
Preserved on parchment
To be read, kept alive,
Time and time again.
As we mortals waste away—
As we age—our minds, our bodies,
Only our souls are immortal
And our souls will continue to remember
The immortal blazons of love
And, in turn, have hope
That true love is also immortal.

A Cricket's Song

Starts at dusk—

Lasts until the newborn morning sun
Sleepily stretches its body over the
        tops of the still, slumbering palms
That frantically cling to
The remaining shreds of darkness
As it silently slips away with the
Stars, as they tiptoe behind the moon,
While it slowly descends
Behind its curtain of bold daylight.

Dusk—

All of the creatures of the night
Slowly creep out of their
        daytime hiding places
And crowd around upon twigs
        and branches to hear
The sweet, shrill tunes
Powered by long legs
        and shimmering wings;
The animals dance
        to the hauntingly captivating
        music.
They swirl and spin in perfect
        rhythm with each other.

The soulful chirping
        carries on until dawn,
Never tiring, never stopping once
        to compose a silence so thick,
That if stopped, that wonderful
        chirping would surely be crushed.
So, on the cricket sings,
A concert for his audience,
        creatures and humans alike,

Ceasing not until the daybreak
    noise begins to fill the
    empty silence.

Careful, Don't Cut Too Deep

A split second
Is all it takes
To make a decision
And make an incision.
The agony that slices through reality
Cuts like a blade through skin,
Through flesh,
Through nerves,
Through veins and arteries.
The life flowing from a simple
      wound
Cannot return;
There is no second chance
To make things right,
No way to turn back
If you change your mind,
No way out of the dark void
That quietly rushes in.

Storm Front

Lightning, thunder... I surrender.
The storm gods rumble over
Electricity on the breeze,
Current touches my fingertips;
Body tingles as
Lightning forks
Spark above mountains of clouds.
Drops of life splatter
Against a dying world,
Giving verve once again
To wilted desolation
In the sweltering summer night.
Building, growling, growing
In a moment of release,
The storm has arrived.
It is done.

Night

Night approaches,
floats in like a mist on stardust.
It covers everything, like a shroud
over the rigorous corpse of the world.

At night, the fairies sleep
while demons roam the dark,
an unseeing void
plaguing our sleep and entering our
dreams, raping our minds,
our subconscious;
the one location we thought was safe
is now a prison of torture
for the masochist,
a tourniquet for the addict,
a match for the firebug,
a morgue for the necrophile,
deliciously possessing our memories
and learning our darkest thoughts
as if to cast a film inside our heads,
a play of the darkest and most forbidden
desires that only we can understand.

At night, the sidewalk is
not quite so warm, and I am
able to walk upon the cement,
my feet bare,
to stand in the open air
as warm and cool
wisps of tantalizing breeze
swirl around my body like
a cloak about a Count,
protecting me, caressing my bare skin
like the hands of a gentle lover,
tickling the hairs on my arms and
tangling sweetly the hair on my head…
winds that whisper in my ear

the secrets and thoughts of people
known and unknown alike.

At night, the Indian summer heat is
not so sweltering,
but the scent of fresh-cut grass and
tree sap are still prominent,
and the odor of sweat still hangs
in the air
like the cruel reminder of an
unspoken threat that dries
the moisture from our eyes
and makes us blink spasmodically
to clear our vision.

At night, our spirits
are free to soar and swoop
through the midnight stillness,
to speak with the night things
of unknown dreams, to run through
fields and get lost in the glory of
the tall, thin stalks that
whisper to them as they pass.

At night, lovers meet
and greet each other
like long lost friends;
they stroll under the stars, the moon,
whispering sweet nothings and
promises in each others' ears
as they lie together and
become one wherever they may.
What matters to them is that
they are finally where they
were meant to be.

At night, mysterious beings
float through our dreams
and the wings of stardust

flap and swirl to cool the
warm night air,
where the smells of the day
still linger in spaces as they
leap and twirl over the
bodies of young lovers that
lay under the vast, dark sky,
under the bright circle of moon,
where at last everyone and
everything may find some peace.

Welcome to the Hellmouth

The street lights
Wink in and out
      of the trees
That line the darkened streets.
As young bloods run
      underneath the glow,
Their oily skin awash
      in the pale orange rays
Like a bath that they've missed
      in their broken-down homes,
In a town of guns and
      violence and no sanctuary.
The power lines sway
      in the cold March wind,
      buzzing with their
Stale current
Flowing to houses with
      stolen cable television
As the stars hide behind
      grey clouds that hold
      no rain, only smoke.
Smoke from burning lands and
      burning homes and
      burning factories and
      burning drugs.
As Florida snow falls to the ground
      in a thick, black blanket
That soils our cars and hair
      and drains the rest of
      the life out of our
      agricultural town,
Sucking the life from our souls
      bit by bit
The longer we stay here.

Wake Up

Something is coming.
Something is about to happen,
I can feel it.
In my head, in my bones.
In my dreams, even.

I can feel it,
Can't you?
Tiny tendrils of
        intuition snaking
        in between your
        thoughts,
Seeping in and pooling,
Finding the weak spots
        in your armor of
        delusion and denial.

Love Immortal

I breathe… the tangy air around me,
It smells of you and me
And the night.
I see… the full moon above us
And the stars that stud the blanket
Wrapped around our bodies.
I hear… the wind in the trees
And in our ears,
The whispers of our undying love.
I taste… the spark of your flame
When our lips meet,
When our souls meet,
When we fly.
I feel… everything;
My head splashed with visions
Of the past, all pasts
And all futures,
We are bound;
Ageless, immortal.

We All Fall Down

Ashes to ashes
Dust to dust
Each day we strive
To do what we must

Each day we sweat
And cry and bleed
Each day we all die
To remain true to our creed

A lack of faith
But abundance of religion
They walk hand in hand
So why the division?

Put down your prejudice
Step back from foolish pride
Confront your fears
There's no reason to hide

Bury your hate
And murder this madness
Look up at the clouds
They weep tears of sadness

How many will suffer
Before our minds come about?
How much longer will we last
Before time runs out?

Bless the souls of your enemies
Repay them with kindness
Then may they see
And regret their blindness

The blood has been shed
The damage is done
None of us will survive
Not a single one

This is Not the Path I Sought

Winter's storm clouds
descend like a cape
over the world
on this moonless night,
a shroud of darkness
hiding the starlight…
the radioactive glow
of the street light
sinister as it bounces
off the trees,
the road signs,
the orange light
sucking up the darkness;
peaceful shimmer destroyed,
life… gone.
Where did it go?

Descent

There must be some way
out of here,
an escape or a lantern
to light the way
out of this faded blue-jean dream
that is supposedly my reality.
All I can see for days
is fog,
skies of grey…
where is my silver lining?
Everything is like an old
Black and white photo
that's been long since forgotten,
put away somewhere in
an old musty box,
just out of reach.

Blue

Bad dreams grow
from blue carpet,
blue carpet on shadowed stairs
       (bad stairs)…
not supposed to go upstairs
       (Mommy's upstairs)…
don't go up there
       (I can feel her, she's upset).
I can't go up, they'll hurt me.

This world… too fragile,
this is not my world.
How do I survive?
Sunshine at the front door,
I see what's in the darkness.

Insight is small solace.

I Don't Have To

This is the space
That I would use
To tell you
All the things
That you already know
That you already feel
The same as I

Sensitivity

Some days the light
        shines
Just a little too bright,
Voices just a bit too loud,
        just a bit too sharp
For me to focus on them.
Some days everything
        just isn't fuzzy
            enough for my tolerance.

Bits & Pieces

Memory
Comes and goes,
Not so much like
        Waves;
Waves are too…
          Consistent.
More like an orbit,
        an ellipse—
Sometimes I remember
        flashes,
Bits and pieces.
Once in a while a new one
          pops up.
I'm starting to remember,
But do I really want to?

The Morning After

The taste of your memory
on my lips, sweet like honey,
lingers long after the
morning sun rises
and steals away
the lingering dew drops
from the blades of grass
that are silently crushed
beneath my feet
as I walk through the
recollection of your touch,
your kiss, your sigh…
my heart feels as though
it could soar
past the trees,
past the clouds,
and through the stars
'til I reach the farthest one.

Shadow on the Wall

He lurks in the darkness
Just beyond the light,
Hovering in the air
Like a hawk stalking prey,
Almost close enough to grasp
But not quite close enough.
Was he ever really there?
Just a shadow on the wall,
A tiny wisp of smoke
From a washed out forest fire;
Just a ghost of a memory
Half-forgotten in the attic,
A trace of a dream
That should have been remembered,
A dark spot in a dark world…
Just a shadow on the wall.

Falling

'Cross the floor
over the pile of clothes
in the queen-size
I lay, skin and soul bare
for you and none other to see.
Your whisper brushes
across my skin
like your soft fingertips,
your breath at my back
when we sleep,
your arms and legs
tangled with mine,
drying sweat
clinging to our hair,
our eyes damp
with exhaustion…
I sigh
and fall into
the peaceful abyss.

Just Me and the Frogs

Chain smoking cowboy killers,
The constriction of blood vessels
Organizes my racing thoughts.
I sit... this broken chair
Is my temple, my haven.
Gazing up
At a cloud-blemished night sky,
I drift in the twisting nether...
I ponder and wait
Until I am once again
Blessed by your presence.
As chaos and foreign smoke
Surround me,
I brace myself against
The cool, hostile breeze
And the toxic lamplight glow.
Anxious, I await the moment
That I may shed this loneliness
That imprisons my soul.
Tobacco stains my vision
And I gaze down at
Smudges,
The birthmark of an artist.
My insomnia fuels
My pen.
The dry spell shattered,
I finish one last cigarette.

Soul Erotica

Watch, my love,
As my body unfolds,
Blossoms
Beneath your miraculous
Fingertips,
Your whispered kiss.

Feel, my love,
As the heat
Of our bodies together
Rises, intensifies
With each breath
And our bodies
Become slick with
Sweat and
Juices from our inferno.

Listen, my love,
As I ache with pleasure
As you plunge
Into my depths at last,
The feel of your
Everything inside me,
My gasps and moans,
My sighs peaking
With every thrust,
My fingers digging in
To your wondrous flesh.

Taste, my love,
My skin,
My frenzied kisses,
My ecstatic explosion,
The electric shudder
Of my body as the final
Recoil of my orgasm
Assaults my spine.

Sigh, my love,
Along with me
As our pulses, beating together,
Slowly return to normal
As we lay together
In the glow of each other;
We breathlessly whisper
Those three words
That mean close to
Nothing
Compared to what
We feel for each other.

She

(She's) kind of like
that asshole kid
on the playground
holding the ropes
at double-dutch,
in her own universe
while the game starts
without her,
dreaming of places she
might fit in better;
sidelong glances and
whispers they think
she won't hear…
she's not like the rest;
everyone can see
and they fear her old soul.

Succubus

Had I the power
Of all the stars in the
Vast carpet of sky,
I would take my soul
And place it next to you
While you dream
So that I may listen
To your beautiful heart
Beating,
So close to mine
Yet so far away.

How I long to feel
Your soft lips 'gainst mine;
To have your calloused hands
Touch me and ignite
A forest fire inside my soul;
To feel your words, lovely words,
Brush across my skin
Like a cool breeze;
To hear your breath,
So filled with desire,
At my throat.

To feel you inside me,
Soul and all, filling me to bursting;
To have you hold me close,
Hug me so tightly
That I might break in your arms,
Fill me with love and passion
So hot that the
Walls catch flame.
Only a matter of time.

Downward Spiral

Stuck in
this cycle,
getting lost
in my own
head again,
grasping
at survival.

Need
something
to dull the
edges
of this
reality
that I'm
not fit for.

This is Not the Road I Thought

I sit…
In my booth,
Nursing my bottomless cup
       of coffee
And smoking a pack of Marbs.
I just need to be by myself,
Just me and Denny's;
Quality time to think,
To collect,
To write my insane
       little heart out.

Enemy

I'm not the one who
> wants to be your enemy;

I'm not the one
> trying to change you,

So don't you dare
> take your anger out on me.

Don't hurt me
> just because I'm standing

With no one else around me
> to take the blame.

I've spent too much of
> my time

Sitting around in silence,
> in fear of you.

Damaged

Damaged, dirty girl,
Abuse and conditioning…
Sometimes she can't
      get off without
         a little bit of pain,
         a little bit of shame.
Born damaged
Or molded that way?
She is what she is
And she's happy that way.

Cuts

I wear this
immortal ache
as I wear my skin.
It is with me always
like the air that
I breathe.
The knife in my heart   (hand)
Twists as the clock
ticks
the seconds of the moments   (years)
away.
One second for
each tear that drops
from my lashes
to the earth below.
One second for
each drop of blood
that flows from my soul   (veins)

I am already dead.

A Denny's Poem

An ashtray of thoughts
Burnt up and flicked away,
Like scattered whispers in the fog,
Though long forgotten, still smolder,
Heat residue from a banked flame.
Dying slow by graves of old,
The recoil of almost nothing
As it slips past your ears
And into the darkness,
Flowing freely from your lips.
Silent, unnoticed prayers of salvation,
Unheard and unhinged in the
      midst of… monotonous turmoil.
An invisible scream,
A forgotten echo as it vibrates
Through the canyons of my psyche,
Elusive images prancing,
Dancing across the desert plains
      of suffocating imagination.
Hollow vignettes trace patterns
Throughout the forest of my vision;
A lost hope, an intangible dream.
Ideas that flow,
Grow in their hurried rush
Like bullets from an anonymous
      gun,
Shadows from an anonymous
      sun…
Linger a while longer before
Flicking this away
Into your ashtray of thoughts.

A Breakthrough

It has been months…
Seems like it has been
Ages…
Since I have last written.
My mind has been blank,
A barren tree,
Unable to bear summer fruit.
Blank pages are
An agonizing void,
A black hole in my spirit,
Sucking everything in
Yet bringing nothing forth.
Absence of word has caused
A miscarriage upon these pages,
With nothing to fill
The lines of life.
I am a malnourished fledgling,
Growing weaker
Each day that passes
And I do not feed.
Grossly underweight pages,
A skeletal vignette upon my soul.
Suddenly! Finally!
Somewhere
In the depths of the night,
A lamp burns
And a page is filled…
I no longer starve to find words
To clothe this naked landscape.

This is Not the Dream I Bought

Lying...
awake in your arms,
I stare at the ceiling,
at the stars beyond.
I realize...
in the faded darkness of our room
as moonbeams cast grey shadows
on the floor,
I am an empty shell, a hollow
excuse for a soul... wandering
aimlessly through (whose?) life.

The Cycle

I think I understand
        Now...
Your misery too much
        for you,
You had to lash out
        in your impotent rage.
Were we reminders
        of some of your own
        personal trauma?
O harbinger of my
        nightmares,
Yes, I think I understand
        now.

Coffee Camping Solo

There were only
        two of us,
Me… and some balding
        middle-aged man
That kept watching me
        through the group of
Obnoxious drunk people
        between us.

Then a massive
        afro-limo-driver
Walked in and sat down.
He said he would take
        his food to go.

Two elderly men
        walked in…
The younger-looking of the two
Looked at me and smiled.
He said to me: "Don't worry,
        young lady,
Everything'll work out fine."

Realization and Denial

Sanctuary and solace
In a place where
People wish impossible wishes
And window-shop for religion.
I stare at the reflection
Of the neon clock in the window
And wonder why my coffee went cold,
And I wish that
If I poured it back into the pot
And warmed it up,
That it wouldn't taste like
      a lost cause.
Yet, maybe if I put in
      just enough sugar,
It might just turn out alright.

I Sense Something is Amiss

What a night is this
that I can actually feel
time beat in my ears
like a leaky faucet
in the dead of night,
and no matter how hard
I try to ignore the drip,
it keeps me awake,
staring at the ceiling
as if all the unanswered questions—and
unquestioned answers—
were glaring back down at me,
daring me to sleep,
daring me to close
just one eyelid
as though the second I wasn't looking
they'd slither away, those niggling thoughts
escaping me, lost forever,
wisps of smoke
from an extinguished candle.

Gaslight

Goodbye...
You are not what you
        claimed you were.
Liar. Thief. Abuser.
Gaslight me into believing
Everything is *my* fault,
Use my insecurities, my own
        mind against me,
To get what you want,
To get your thrill.
To hell with you!
I am no longer your entertainment.

Hindsight (is Always 20/20)

Such a shame…
I didn't notice when you
Stopped kissing me
Like you meant it
Until I wasted
Far too many years
On you.

Just a Fever of Fate I've Caught

Your words
A lingering poison
     in my veins
Bone shards piercing
     my brain
Trying to burrow
     deeper to find
     a handhold
My scars an invisible
     reminder:
Trust no one.

Restless

I sat down in the chaise lounge,
read my nails and painted a book;
got up,
turned the TV on and back off,
took a walk in my trench coat and bare feet.
I threw the laundry in the shower
and blared "Me and Bobby McGee,"
played rook and spider webs in my head,
spilled coffee on the cat's tail,
and stepped on the keyboard.

This silent house is making me sane;
I walk into the sunshine with my umbrella
(you never know when the gods are going to spit);
sometimes the sound of goodbye
is louder than any drumbeat.
I slam the windows and shut the door
on my way into the chaos;
I walk out of your world and into mine
with nothing to gain
and everything to leave behind.

You were someone I used to think I knew,
and now you've sauntered into my bubble
and turned my world wrong side up.

Free

Free spirit I am
And have always been.
Cut my own path,
Ignoring the looks, the whispers
      (that girl is strange…),
Longing for acceptance,
Some place to fit in.
Ostracized by my own
      individuality,
My refusal to submit, to mold
      myself into something I am not.
Cut my own path, I did;
Tooth and nail, most of the way.
Yet I survived,
A free spirit still,
And ever will I be.

Moving On

Smothered
for far too long,
Hiding
behind fear
and distrust…

Do I dare
allow myself
To be
vulnerable again?

La passion

Hands, lips, limbs
All tangled.
Teeth, bruises,
Stubbled skin.
Wound inside
Our bubble,
Safe from the
Outside world.
No one else
Can come in.

Chameleon Girl

Fragile girl… adapt.
Must adapt to survive,
Automatically absorbing
Bits and pieces
Of souls that make an impression.
Alien girl…
Trapped in this 'verse,
Shell-shocked and wandering,
Wondering,
Are there any parallels better?
Are they all just as fucked somehow?
Chameleon girl…
Blending for decades,
Growing, adapting
A new desire,
Not just to survive,
       but to… thrive?
Old habit armor;
What shall be your weapon of choice,
Warrior girl?

Sanctuary

Your eyes
So open, so full of emotion,
So innocent in your expressions—
Almost child-like in your joy,
Sometimes near painful
To look for too long,
Yet I find myself drawn in
Over and over.
You surround me, envelope me in
Something… (a blanket,
      or a bubble, perhaps)
That shuts the world out,
That makes the monsters go away.
You are my solace,
My sanctuary.
To describe what you do
To me, for me; I lose purchase
In my ability to voice or verse
That which is in mine heart.
Pray this be love truly,
For I am already too far gone.

The Compatibility Culmination

Tiny supernovas
In the black,
I pry my gaze away
Just to catch my breath.
You put my pieces
Back together
So well that they
Almost fit…
The missing pieces
Were ill-fitting, anyway.
Your soul—the cement
That keeps me whole—
And the more I see of it,
The more I fall
In love with you.

Pestilence

Time will expose you
for the vermin that you are:
the lies, the manipulation—
your deceit
will come full circle.

Parasite;
your infestation has
been expunged.
Go leech and poison
some other pathetic soul.

Spark

That night, I touched
        your hand
And I saw sparks,
Felt them
        behind my eyes,
And my heart
        recognized
That you needed me
        as much as I
        needed you.

Hollow Dolly

Hollow Dolly has
Found her viscera
Somewhere over yonder.
Stunted trees
Belie iron taproots,
Strengthen her walls and
      roof overhead.
Forgiveness and closure, ammo in
Her war against herself.

Skinny Bitch

I am
a skinny bitch
and I am not sorry.

Go ahead
and hate me;
I really don't care.

I have
hated my body
just as much as you.

And I
have hurt myself
far more than you ever could.

It's just
the way I
was made, just like you.

And I
have no more
control over it than you.

So you
should learn to
be happy in your own skin.

I am
still learning, but
I have made such progress.

So yes,
I am a
skinny bitch. So what?

Dad

Years have passed
Since you departed
And even more
Since we have spoken

I miss you like
Only family does
Even though
We were broken

I Hope it Was Worth It

Once in a while,
Your words
Float through my memory.

I had to
Take the chance;
I couldn't ignore the feeling.

And taking the risk
Of being a rebound
Was really your own doing.

Now hindsight has proven
Time and time again, that yes…
It was fucking worth it.

Beautiful Host

The land has begun
        its rebellion
Against our parasitic
        invasion.
An infestation to be
        burned away by wildfire,
Squelched in a flood
        of rage…
We who wage war
        with ourselves
Crack the world open and
        steal her bones.
For what? For greed?
For power? For destruction?
We are a pestilence;
We do not deserve this
        beautiful host.

About the Author

Naomi Smith, 32, was born in the small town of Pahokee, where the muck of South Florida breeds more than one kind of talent. A literary enthusiast since early childhood, Naomi wrote her first poem at the age of 10 and hasn't stopped since.

After being stationed in the Pacific Northwest during her brief stint in the United States Air Force, Naomi found breathtaking Western Washington the ideal place to set down her eclectic roots and cultivate inspiration.

www.ingramcontent.com/pod-product-compliance
Lightning Source LLC
Chambersburg PA
CBHW071722040426
42446CB00011B/2174